A Cello Advent

25 Days of Christmas Solos and Duets for a Most Joyous Season

Book One

Myanna Harvey and Cassia Harvey

Cover Image
The Miriam and Ira D. Wallach Division of Art, Prints and Photographs: Picture Collection, The New York Public Library. "Christmas greetings." The New York Public Library Digital Collections. https://digitalcollections.nypl.org/items/510d47e3-6f8c-a3d9-e040-e00a18064a99

CHP433

©2022 C. Harvey Publications®
All Rights Reserved.
www.charveypublications.com - print books
www.learnstrings.com - downloadable books
www.harveystringarrangements.com - chamber music

Table of Contents

Page

How the Book Works..................................3
Dec. 1: The First Noel..............................4
Dec. 2: We Three Kings..............................6
Dec. 3: Good King Wenceslas.........................8
Dec. 4: Go, Tell It on the Mountain................10
Dec. 5: Jingle Bells...............................12
Dec. 6: O Come, All Ye Faithful....................16
Dec. 7: Away in a Manger...........................18
Dec. 8: O Christmas Tree...........................20
Dec. 9: Angels We Have Heard on High...............22
Dec. 10: Up on the Housetop........................26
Dec. 11: God Rest Ye, Merry Gentlemen..............28
Dec. 12: O Little Town of Bethlehem................30
Dec. 13: I Saw Three Ships.........................32
Dec. 14: March from **The Nutcracker**.............34
Dec. 15: What Child is This........................38
Dec. 16: O Holy Night..............................42
Dec. 17: O Come, O Come Emmanuel...................46
Dec. 18: The Twelve Days of Christmas..............48
Dec. 19: Carol of the Bells........................52
Dec. 20: Deck the Halls............................54
Dec. 21: Hark, the Herald Angels Sing..............56
Dec. 22: Waltz from **The Nutcracker**.............58
Dec. 23: Joy to the World..........................62
Dec. 24: Silent Night..............................64
Dec. 25: We Wish You a Merry Christmas.............66

December 1st: Warm-Up for The First Noel

C. Harvey

December 1st Melody: The First Noel

Traditional French Carol

How the Book Works

This book can work as a music advent calendar, giving you warm-up exercises, melodies, and variations on carols to play on the days leading up to Christmas.

On each day of December, you can play a warm-up, then the melody, and finally work on the variation. Then, you can play the melodies and variations with cello duet parts at a lesson or a chamber music session.

Looking to play Christmas music with friends? This book is compatible with the Violin and the Viola books and can be used to play Christmas duets with those instruments as well!

Play-Along Files

Links to available play-along files and videos can be found at www.charveypublications.com/adventplayalong.

Performance Suggestion

When performing from the book, a good way to format a carol would be to play the Melody, the Variation, and then the Melody again.

Please note: Playing the Melody simultaneously with another player playing the Variation is not recommended.

Free Sheet Music from C. Harvey Publications!

Free exercises, solos, and duets can be found on our blog at
https://www.charveypublications.com/better-string-playing-blog

Have a Question?

We are here to answer questions about the book! Email us at charveypublications@gmail.com or fill out the contact form here:
https://www.charveypublications.com/contact.html

©2022 C. Harvey Publications® All Rights Reserved.

A Cello Advent, Book One
5

December 1st Variation: The First Noel

M. Harvey, after Traditional Melody

December 1st Duet Part: The First Noel

M. Harvey

©2022 C. Harvey Publications All Rights Reserved.

6

December 2nd: Warm-Up for We Three Kings

C. Harvey

Tremolo: In the upper half of the bow, move the bow back and forth very lightly, and as fast as possible for the length of the note.

December 2nd Melody: We Three Kings

J. Hopkins

Moderato

©2022 C. Harvey Publications All Rights Reserved.

A Cello Advent, Book One

December 2nd Variation: We Three Kings

M. Harvey after J. Hopkins

December 2nd Duet Part: We Three Kings

M. Harvey

©2022 C. Harvey Publications All Rights Reserved.

December 3rd: Warm-Up for Good King Wenceslas

A Cello Advent, Book One
C. Harvey

December 3rd Melody: Good King Wenceslas

Piae Cantones, arr. J. Stainer

©2022 C. Harvey Publications All Rights Reserved.

A Cello Advent, Book One

December 3rd Variation: Good King Wenceslas

M. Harvey, after Piao Cantones

December 3rd Duet Part: Good King Wenceslas

M. Harvey

©2022 C. Harvey Publications All Rights Reserved.

December 4th: Warm-Up for Go, Tell It On the Mountain

C. Harvey

December 4th Melody: Go, Tell It On the Mountain

Moderato

Traditional African-American Spiritual

©2022 C. Harvey Publications All Rights Reserved.

December 5th: Warm-Ups for Jingle Bells

G Major Scale
C. Harvey

G Major Etude
C. Harvey

©2022 C. Harvey Publications All Rights Reserved.

Agility Etude

C. Harvey

14

A Cello Advent, Book One

December 5th Melody: Jingle Bells

J. Pierpont

Allegro

December 5th Variation: Jingle Bells

M. Harvey, after J. Pierpont

Allegro

©2022 C. Harvey Publications All Rights Reserved.

A Cello Advent, Book One

15

December 5th Duet Part: Jingle Bells

M. Harvey

©2022 C. Harvey Publications All Rights Reserved.

A Cello Advent, Book One

December 6th Variation: O Come, All Ye Faithful

M. Harvey, after J. Wade

December 6th Duet Part: O Come, All Ye Faithful

M. Harvey

©2022 C. Harvey Publications All Rights Reserved.

18 A Cello Advent, Book One

December 7th: Warm-Up for Away in a Manger
C. Harvey

December 7th Melody: Away in a Manger
J. Murray

©2022 C. Harvey Publications All Rights Reserved.

A Cello Advent, Book One
19

December 7th Variation: Away in a Manger

M. Harvey, after J. Murray

December 7th Duet Part: Away in a Manger

M. Harvey

©2022 C. Harvey Publications All Rights Reserved.

December 8th: Warm-Up for O Christmas Tree

C. Harvey

December 8th Melody: O Christmas Tree

Traditional Melody

A Cello Advent, Book One

21

December 8th Variation: O Christmas Tree

M. Harvey, after Trad. Melody

December 8th Duet Part: O Christmas Tree

M. Harvey

©2022 C. Harvey Publications All Rights Reserved.

December 9th: Warm-Ups for Angels We Have Heard on High

D Major Scale Etude

C. Harvey

Mordent

is played

String Crossing Etude

C. Harvey

December 9th Melody: Angels We Have Heard on High

Traditional Melody

December 9th Variation: Angels We Have Heard on High

M. Harvey, after Trad. Melody

A Cello Advent, Book One

December 9th Duet Part: Angels We Have Heard on High

M. Harvey

©2022 C. Harvey Publications All Rights Reserved.

December 10th: Warm-Up for Up on the Housetop

C. Harvey

Left-hand pizzicato (use any finger)

December 10th Melody: Up on the Housetop

B. Hanby

Allegro

A Cello Advent, Book One
27

December 10th Variation: Up on the Housetop

M. Harvey, after B. Hanby

December 10th Duet Part: Up on the Housetop

M. Harvey

©2022 C. Harvey Publications All Rights Reserved.

December 11th: Warm-Up for God Rest Ye, Merry Gentlemen

C. Harvey

December 11th Melody: God Rest Ye, Merry Gentlemen

Traditional Melody

December 13th: Warm-Up for I Saw Three Ships

C. Harvey

December 13th Melody: I Saw Three Ships

Traditional Melody

©2022 C. Harvey Publications All Rights Reserved.

December 13th Variation: I Saw Three Ships

December 14th: Warm-Ups for March from *The Nutcracker*

D Major Scale Rhythm No. 1
C. Harvey

D Major Scale Rhythm No. 2
C. Harvey

A Cello Advent, Book One

D Major Rhythm Etude

C. Harvey

C♯ and A♯

C. Harvey

December 14th Melody: March from *The Nutcracker*

P. Tchaikovsky

A Cello Advent, Book One

December 14th Variation: March from *The Nutcracker*

P. Tchaikovsky, arr. M. Harvey

Tempo di Marcia

December 14th Duet Part: March from *The Nutcracker*

M. Harvey, after P. Tchaikovsky

Tempo di Marcia

©2022 C. Harvey Publications All Rights Reserved.

December 15th: Warm-Ups for What Child Is This

D Minor Etude No. 1

C. Harvey

D Minor Etude No. 2

C. Harvey

December 15th Melody: What Child Is This

Traditional Melody

December 15th Variation: What Child Is This

M. Harvey, after Traditional Melody

December 15th Duet Part: What Child Is This

M. Harvey

December 16th: Warm-Ups for O Holy Night

C Major Etude No. 1

C. Harvey

C Major Etude No. 2

C. Harvey

44

December 16th Melody: O Holy Night

Andante

A. Adam

rit.

December 16th Variation: O Holy Night

Andante

M. Harvey, after A. Adam

A Cello Advent, Book One

©2022 C. Harvey Publications All Rights Reserved.

A Cello Advent, Book One

45

December 16th Duet Part: O Holy Night

M. Harvey

©2022 C. Harvey Publications All Rights Reserved.

December 17th Variation: O Come, O Come Emmanuel

Andante

M. Harvey, after Plainsong

December 17th Duet Part: O Come, O Come Emmanuel

M. Harvey

Andante

December 18th: Warm-Ups for The Twelve Days of Christmas

Twelve Days Bow Rhythm Etude

C. Harvey

Twelve Days Agility Etude

C. Harvey

December 18th Melody: The Twelve Days of Christmas

Traditional Melody

December 18th Variation: The Twelve Days of Christmas

M. Harvey, after Traditional Melody

©2022 C. Harvey Publications All Rights Reserved.

A Cello Advent, Book One

51

December 18th Duet Part: The Twelve Days of Christmas

M. Harvey

©2022 C. Harvey Publications All Rights Reserved.

December 19th: Warm-Up for Carol of the Bells
C. Harvey

December 19th Melody: Carol of the Bells
Allegro

M. Leontovych

©2022 C. Harvey Publications All Rights Reserved.

December 20th: Warm-Up for Deck the Halls

C. Harvey

December 20th Melody: Deck the Halls

T. Oliphant

December 21st: Warm-Up for Hark, the Herald Angels Sing

C. Harvey

December 21st Melody: Hark, the Herald Angels Sing

F. Mendelssohn

Moderato

December 21st Variation: Hark, the Herald Angels Sing

M. Harvey, after F. Mendelssohn

December 21st Duet Part: Hark, the Herald Angels Sing

M. Harvey

©2022 C. Harvey Publications All Rights Reserved.

December 22nd: Warm-Ups for Waltz from *The Nutcracker*

C. Harvey

G# Study

E♯ Study

C. Harvey

Scale Rhythm Study

C. Harvey

December 22nd Melody: Waltz of the Flowers, from *The Nutcracker*

P. Tchaikovsky

Tempo di Valse

December 22nd Variation: Waltz of the Flowers, from *The Nutcracker*

P. Tchaikovsky, arr. M. Harvey

Tempo di Valse

©2022 C. Harvey Publications All Rights Reserved.

A Cello Advent, Book One   61

December 22nd Duet Part: Waltz of the Flowers, from *The Nutcracker*

Tempo di Valse

M. Harvey, after P. Tchaikovsky

A Cello Advent, Book One

63

December 23rd Variation: Joy To the World

M. Harvey, after L. Mason

December 23rd Duet Part: Joy To the World

M. Harvey

©2022 C. Harvey Publications All Rights Reserved.

December 24th: Warm-Up for Silent Night
C. Harvey

December 24th Melody: Silent Night
F. Gruber

©2022 C. Harvey Publications All Rights Reserved.

December 25th: Warm-Up for We Wish You a Merry Christmas

C. Harvey

December 25th Melody: We Wish You a Merry Christmas

Traditional Melody

December 25th Variation: We Wish You a Merry Christmas

M. Harvey, after Traditional Melody

December 25th Duet Part: We Wish You a Merry Christmas

M. Harvey

Available from www.charveypublications.com
The Blackberry Blossom Fiddle Book for Cello CHP385

Fiddle Exercises at two different levels.

Fiddle Tunes at two different levels can be played solo, in duets, or in chamber ensembles.

Exercises, Tunes, and Harmonies are compatible with the violin, viola, and string bass books!